Assessing Russian Activities and Intentions

in Recent US Elections

by

ICA

Intelligence Community Assessment

ISBN: 978-1542410663

Background to "Assessing Russian Activities and Intentions in Recent US Elections": The Analytic Process and Cyber Incident Attribution

6 January 2017

Background to "Assessing Russian Activities and Intentions in Recent US Elections": The Analytic Process and Cyber Incident Attribution

"Assessing Russian Activities and Intentions in Recent US Elections" is a declassified version of a highly classified assessment that has been provided to the President and to recipients approved by the President.

- The Intelligence Community rarely can publicly reveal the full extent of its knowledge or the precise bases for its assessments, as the release of such information would reveal sensitive sources or methods and imperil the ability to collect critical foreign intelligence in the future.

- Thus, while the conclusions in the report are all reflected in the classified assessment, the declassified report does not and cannot include the full supporting information, including specific intelligence and sources and methods.

The Analytic Process

The mission of the Intelligence Community is to seek to reduce the uncertainty surrounding foreign activities, capabilities, or leaders' intentions. This objective is difficult to achieve when seeking to understand complex issues on which foreign actors go to extraordinary lengths to hide or obfuscate their activities.

- On these issues of great importance to US national security, the goal of intelligence analysis is to provide assessments to decisionmakers that are intellectually rigorous, objective, timely, and useful, and that adhere to tradecraft standards.

- The tradecraft standards for analytic products have been refined over the past ten years. These standards include describing sources (including their reliability and access to the information they provide), clearly expressing uncertainty, distinguishing between underlying information and analysts' judgments and assumptions, exploring alternatives, demonstrating relevance to the customer, using strong and transparent logic, and explaining change or consistency in judgments over time.

- Applying these standards helps ensure that the Intelligence Community provides US policymakers, warfighters, and operators with the best and most accurate insight, warning, and context, as well as potential opportunities to advance US national security.

Intelligence Community analysts integrate information from a wide range of sources, including human sources, technical collection, and open source information, and apply specialized skills and structured analytic tools to draw inferences informed by the data available, relevant past activity, and logic and reasoning to provide insight into what is happening and the prospects for the future.

- A critical part of the analyst's task is to explain uncertainties associated with major judgments based on the quantity and quality of the source material, information gaps, and the complexity of the issue.

- When Intelligence Community analysts use words such as "we assess" or "we judge," they are conveying an analytic assessment or judgment.

- Some analytic judgments are based directly on collected information; others rest on previous judgments, which serve as building blocks in rigorous analysis. In either type of judgment, the tradecraft standards outlined above ensure that analysts have an appropriate basis for the judgment.

- Intelligence Community judgments often include two important elements: judgments of how likely it is that something has happened or will happen (using terms such as "likely" or "unlikely") and confidence levels in those judgments (low, moderate, and high) that refer to the evidentiary basis, logic and reasoning, and precedents that underpin the judgments.

Determining Attribution in Cyber Incidents

The nature of cyberspace makes attribution of cyber operations difficult but not impossible. Every kind of cyber operation—malicious or not—leaves a trail. US Intelligence Community analysts use this information, their constantly growing knowledge base of previous events and known malicious actors, and their knowledge of how these malicious actors work and the tools that they use, to attempt to trace these operations back to their source. In every case, they apply the same tradecraft standards described in the Analytic Process above.

- Analysts consider a series of questions to assess how the information compares with existing knowledge and adjust their confidence in their judgments as appropriate to account for any alternative hypotheses and ambiguities.

- An assessment of attribution usually is not a simple statement of who conducted an operation, but rather a series of judgments that describe whether it was an isolated incident, who was the likely perpetrator, that perpetrator's possible motivations, and whether a foreign government had a role in ordering or leading the operation.

This page intentionally left blank.

Scope and Sourcing

Information available as of 29 December 2016 was used in the preparation of this product.

Scope

This report includes an analytic assessment drafted and coordinated among The Central Intelligence Agency (CIA), The Federal Bureau of Investigation (FBI), and The National Security Agency (NSA), which draws on intelligence information collected and disseminated by those three agencies. It covers the motivation and scope of Moscow's intentions regarding US elections and Moscow's use of cyber tools and media campaigns to influence US public opinion. The assessment focuses on activities aimed at the 2016 US presidential election and draws on our understanding of previous Russian influence operations. When we use the term "we" it refers to an assessment by all three agencies.

- This report is a declassified version of a highly classified assessment. This document's conclusions are identical to the highly classified assessment, but this document does not include the full supporting information, including specific intelligence on key elements of the influence campaign. Given the redactions, we made minor edits purely for readability and flow.

We did not make an assessment of the impact that Russian activities had on the outcome of the 2016 election. The US Intelligence Community is charged with monitoring and assessing the intentions, capabilities, and actions of foreign actors; it does not analyze US political processes or US public opinion.

- New information continues to emerge, providing increased insight into Russian activities.

Sourcing

Many of the key judgments in this assessment rely on a body of reporting from multiple sources that are consistent with our understanding of Russian behavior. Insights into Russian efforts—including specific cyber operations—and Russian views of key US players derive from multiple corroborating sources.

Some of our judgments about Kremlin preferences and intent are drawn from the behavior of Kremlin-loyal political figures, state media, and pro-Kremlin social media actors, all of whom the Kremlin either directly uses to convey messages or who are answerable to the Kremlin. The Russian leadership invests significant resources in both foreign and domestic propaganda and places a premium on transmitting what it views as consistent, self-reinforcing narratives regarding its desires and redlines, whether on Ukraine, Syria, or relations with the United States.

Assessing Russian Activities and Intentions in Recent US Elections

ICA 2017-01D
6 January 2017

Key Judgments

Russian efforts to influence the 2016 US presidential election represent the most recent expression of Moscow's longstanding desire to undermine the US-led liberal democratic order, but these activities demonstrated a significant escalation in directness, level of activity, and scope of effort compared to previous operations.

We assess Russian President Vladimir Putin ordered an influence campaign in 2016 aimed at the US presidential election. Russia's goals were to undermine public faith in the US democratic process, denigrate Secretary Clinton, and harm her electability and potential presidency. We further assess Putin and the Russian Government developed a clear preference for President-elect Trump. We have high confidence in these judgments.

- **We also assess Putin and the Russian Government aspired to help President-elect Trump's election chances when possible by discrediting Secretary Clinton and publicly contrasting her unfavorably to him.** All three agencies agree with this judgment. CIA and FBI have high confidence in this judgment; NSA has moderate confidence.

- Moscow's approach evolved over the course of the campaign based on Russia's understanding of the electoral prospects of the two main candidates. When it appeared to Moscow that Secretary Clinton was likely to win the election, the Russian influence campaign began to focus more on undermining her future presidency.

- Further information has come to light since Election Day that, when combined with Russian behavior since early November 2016, increases our confidence in our assessments of Russian motivations and goals.

Moscow's influence campaign followed a Russian messaging strategy that blends covert intelligence operations—such as cyber activity—with overt efforts by Russian Government agencies, state-funded media, third-party intermediaries, and paid social media users or "trolls." Russia, like its Soviet predecessor, has a history of conducting covert influence campaigns focused on US presidential elections that have used intelligence officers and agents and press placements to disparage candidates perceived as hostile to the Kremlin.

- Russia's intelligence services conducted cyber operations against targets associated with the 2016 US presidential election, including targets associated with both major US political parties.

- We assess with high confidence that Russian military intelligence (General Staff Main Intelligence Directorate or GRU) used the Guccifer 2.0 persona and DCLeaks.com to release US victim data obtained in cyber operations publicly and in exclusives to media outlets and relayed material to WikiLeaks.

- Russian intelligence obtained and maintained access to elements of multiple US state or local electoral boards. **DHS assesses that the types of systems Russian actors targeted or compromised were not involved in vote tallying.**

- Russia's state-run propaganda machine contributed to the influence campaign by serving as a platform for Kremlin messaging to Russian and international audiences.

We assess Moscow will apply lessons learned from its Putin-ordered campaign aimed at the US presidential election to future influence efforts worldwide, including against US allies and their election processes.

Contents

Scope and Sourcing   i

Key Judgments   ii

Contents   iv

CIA/FBI/NSA Assessment: Russia's Influence Campaign Targeting the 2016 US Presidential Election

Putin Ordered Campaign To Influence US Election   1

Russian Campaign Was Multifaceted   2

Influence Effort Was Boldest Yet in the US   5

Election Operation Signals "New Normal" in Russian Influence Efforts   5

Annexes

A: Russia—Kremlin's TV Seeks To Influence Politics, Fuel Discontent in US   6

B: Estimative Language   13

Russia's Influence Campaign Targeting the 2016 US Presidential Election

Russia's Influence Campaign Targeting the 2016 US Presidential Election

Putin Ordered Campaign To Influence US Election

We assess with high confidence that Russian President Vladimir Putin ordered an influence campaign in 2016 aimed at the US presidential election, the consistent goals of which were to undermine public faith in the US democratic process, denigrate Secretary Clinton, and harm her electability and potential presidency. We further assess Putin and the Russian Government developed a clear preference for President-elect Trump. When it appeared to Moscow that Secretary Clinton was likely to win the election, the Russian influence campaign then focused on undermining her expected presidency.

- We also assess Putin and the Russian Government aspired to help President-elect Trump's election chances when possible by discrediting Secretary Clinton and publicly contrasting her unfavorably to him. All three agencies agree with this judgment. CIA and FBI have high confidence in this judgment; NSA has moderate confidence.

- In trying to influence the US election, we assess the Kremlin sought to advance its longstanding desire to undermine the US-led liberal democratic order, the promotion of which Putin and other senior Russian leaders view as a threat to Russia and Putin's regime.

- Putin publicly pointed to the Panama Papers disclosure and the Olympic doping scandal as US-directed efforts to defame Russia, suggesting he sought to use disclosures to discredit the image of the United States and cast it as hypocritical.

- Putin most likely wanted to discredit Secretary Clinton because he has publicly blamed her since 2011 for inciting mass protests against his regime in late 2011 and early 2012, and because he holds a grudge for comments he almost certainly saw as disparaging him.

We assess Putin, his advisers, and the Russian Government developed a clear preference for President-elect Trump over Secretary Clinton.

- Beginning in June, Putin's public comments about the US presidential race avoided directly praising President-elect Trump, probably because Kremlin officials thought that any praise from Putin personally would backfire in the United States. Nonetheless, Putin publicly indicated a preference for President-elect Trump's stated policy to work with Russia, and pro-Kremlin figures spoke highly about what they saw as his Russia-friendly positions on Syria and Ukraine. Putin publicly contrasted the President-elect's approach to Russia with Secretary Clinton's "aggressive rhetoric."

- Moscow also saw the election of President-elect Trump as a way to achieve an international counterterrorism coalition against the Islamic State in Iraq and the Levant (ISIL).

- Putin has had many positive experiences working with Western political leaders whose business interests made them more disposed to deal with Russia, such as former Italian Prime Minister Silvio Berlusconi and former German Chancellor Gerhard Schroeder.

- Putin, Russian officials, and other pro-Kremlin pundits stopped publicly criticizing the US election process as unfair almost immediately after the election because Moscow probably assessed it would be counterproductive to building positive relations.

We assess the influence campaign aspired to help President-elect Trump's chances of victory when possible by discrediting Secretary Clinton and publicly contrasting her unfavorably to the President-elect. When it appeared to Moscow that Secretary Clinton was likely to win the presidency the Russian influence campaign focused more on undercutting Secretary Clinton's legitimacy and crippling her presidency from its start, including by impugning the fairness of the election.

- Before the election, Russian diplomats had publicly denounced the US electoral process and were prepared to publicly call into question the validity of the results. Pro-Kremlin bloggers had prepared a Twitter campaign, #DemocracyRIP, on election night in anticipation of Secretary Clinton's victory, judging from their social media activity.

Russian Campaign Was Multifaceted

Moscow's use of disclosures during the US election was unprecedented, but its influence campaign otherwise followed a longstanding Russian messaging strategy that blends covert intelligence operations—such as cyber activity—with overt efforts by Russian Government agencies, state-funded media, third-party intermediaries, and paid social media users or "trolls."

- We assess that influence campaigns are approved at the highest levels of the Russian Government—particularly those that would be politically sensitive.

- Moscow's campaign aimed at the US election reflected years of investment in its capabilities, which Moscow has honed in the former Soviet states.

- By their nature, Russian influence campaigns are multifaceted and designed to be deniable because they use a mix of agents of influence, cutouts, front organizations, and false-flag operations. Moscow demonstrated this during the Ukraine crisis in 2014, when Russia deployed forces and advisers to eastern Ukraine and denied it publicly.

The Kremlin's campaign aimed at the US election featured disclosures of data obtained through Russian cyber operations; intrusions into US state and local electoral boards; and overt propaganda. Russian intelligence collection both informed and enabled the influence campaign.

Cyber Espionage Against US Political Organizations. Russia's intelligence services conducted cyber operations against targets associated with the 2016 US presidential election, including targets associated with both major US political parties.

We assess Russian intelligence services collected against the US primary campaigns, think tanks, and lobbying groups they viewed as likely to shape future US policies. In July 2015, Russian intelligence gained access to Democratic National Committee (DNC) networks and maintained that access until at least June 2016.

- The General Staff Main Intelligence Directorate (GRU) probably began cyber operations aimed at the US election by March 2016. We assess that the GRU operations resulted in the compromise of the personal e-mail accounts of Democratic Party officials and political figures. By May, the GRU had exfiltrated large volumes of data from the DNC.

Public Disclosures of Russian-Collected Data. We assess with high confidence that the GRU used the Guccifer 2.0 persona, DCLeaks.com, and WikiLeaks to release US victim data obtained in cyber operations publicly and in exclusives to media outlets.

- Guccifer 2.0, who claimed to be an independent Romanian hacker, made multiple contradictory statements and false claims about his likely Russian identity throughout the election. Press reporting suggests more than one person claiming to be Guccifer 2.0 interacted with journalists.

- Content that we assess was taken from e-mail accounts targeted by the GRU in March 2016 appeared on DCLeaks.com starting in June.

We assess with high confidence that the GRU relayed material it acquired from the DNC and senior Democratic officials to WikiLeaks. Moscow most likely chose WikiLeaks because of its self-proclaimed reputation for authenticity. Disclosures through WikiLeaks did not contain any evident forgeries.

- In early September, Putin said publicly it was important the DNC data was exposed to WikiLeaks, calling the search for the source of the leaks a distraction and denying Russian "state-level" involvement.

- The Kremlin's principal international propaganda outlet RT (formerly Russia Today) has actively collaborated with WikiLeaks. RT's editor-in-chief visited WikiLeaks founder Julian Assange at the Ecuadorian Embassy in London in August 2013, where they discussed renewing his broadcast contract with RT, according to Russian and Western media. Russian media subsequently announced that RT had become "the only Russian media company" to partner with WikiLeaks and had received access to "new leaks of secret information." RT routinely gives Assange sympathetic coverage and provides him a platform to denounce the United States.

These election-related disclosures reflect a pattern of Russian intelligence using hacked information in targeted influence efforts against targets such as Olympic athletes and other foreign governments. Such efforts have included releasing or altering personal data, defacing websites, or releasing e-mails.

- A prominent target since the 2016 Summer Olympics has been the World Anti-Doping Agency (WADA), with leaks that we assess to have originated with the GRU and that have involved data on US athletes.

Russia collected on some Republican-affiliated targets but did not conduct a comparable disclosure campaign.

Russian Cyber Intrusions Into State and Local Electoral Boards. Russian intelligence accessed elements of multiple state or local electoral boards. Since early 2014, Russian intelligence has researched US electoral processes and related technology and equipment.

- DHS assesses that the types of systems we observed Russian actors targeting or compromising are not involved in vote tallying.

Russian Propaganda Efforts. Russia's state-run propaganda machine—comprised of its domestic media apparatus, outlets targeting global audiences such as RT and Sputnik, and a network of quasi-government trolls—contributed to the influence campaign by serving as a platform for Kremlin messaging to Russian and international audiences. State-owned Russian media made increasingly favorable comments about President-elect Trump as the 2016 US general and primary election campaigns progressed while consistently offering negative coverage of Secretary Clinton.

- Starting in March 2016, Russian Government–linked actors began openly supporting President-elect Trump's candidacy in media aimed at English-speaking audiences. RT and Sputnik—another government-funded outlet producing pro-Kremlin radio and online content in a variety of languages for international audiences—consistently cast President-elect Trump as the target of unfair coverage from traditional US media outlets that they claimed were subservient to a corrupt political establishment.

- Russian media hailed President-elect Trump's victory as a vindication of Putin's advocacy of global populist movements—the theme of Putin's annual conference for Western academics in October 2016—and the latest example of Western liberalism's collapse.

- Putin's chief propagandist Dmitriy Kiselev used his flagship weekly newsmagazine program this fall to cast President-elect Trump as an outsider victimized by a corrupt political establishment and faulty democratic election process that aimed to prevent his election because of his desire to work with Moscow.

- Pro-Kremlin proxy Vladimir Zhirinovskiy, leader of the nationalist Liberal Democratic Party of Russia, proclaimed just before the election that if President-elect Trump won, Russia would "drink champagne" in anticipation of being able to advance its positions on Syria and Ukraine.

RT's coverage of Secretary Clinton throughout the US presidential campaign was consistently negative and focused on her leaked e-mails and accused her of corruption, poor physical and mental health, and ties to Islamic extremism. Some Russian officials echoed Russian lines for the influence campaign that Secretary Clinton's election could lead to a war between the United States and Russia.

- In August, Kremlin-linked political analysts suggested avenging negative Western reports on Putin by airing segments devoted to Secretary Clinton's alleged health problems.

- On 6 August, RT published an English-language video called "Julian Assange Special: Do WikiLeaks Have the E-mail That'll Put Clinton in Prison?" and an exclusive interview with Assange entitled "Clinton and ISIS Funded by the Same Money." RT's most popular video on Secretary Clinton, "How 100% of the Clintons' 'Charity' Went to...Themselves," had more than 9 million views on social media platforms. RT's most popular English language video about the President-elect, called "Trump Will Not Be Permitted To Win," featured Assange and had 2.2 million views.

- For more on Russia's past media efforts—including portraying the 2012 US electoral process as undemocratic—please see Annex A: Russia—Kremlin's TV Seeks To Influence Politics, Fuel Discontent in US.

Russia used trolls as well as RT as part of its influence efforts to denigrate Secretary Clinton. This effort amplified stories on scandals about Secretary Clinton and the role of WikiLeaks in the election campaign.

- The likely financier of the so-called Internet Research Agency of professional trolls located in Saint Petersburg is a close Putin ally with ties to Russian intelligence.

- A journalist who is a leading expert on the Internet Research Agency claimed that some social media accounts that appear to be tied to Russia's professional trolls—because they previously were devoted to supporting Russian actions in Ukraine—started to advocate for President-elect Trump as early as December 2015.

Influence Effort Was Boldest Yet in the US

Russia's effort to influence the 2016 US presidential election represented a significant escalation in directness, level of activity, and scope of effort compared to previous operations aimed at US elections. We assess the 2016 influence campaign reflected the Kremlin's recognition of the worldwide effects that mass disclosures of US Government and other private data—such as those conducted by WikiLeaks and others—have achieved in recent years, and their understanding of the value of orchestrating such disclosures to maximize the impact of compromising information.

- During the Cold War, the Soviet Union used intelligence officers, influence agents, forgeries, and press placements to disparage candidates perceived as hostile to the Kremlin, according to a former KGB archivist.

Since the Cold War, Russian intelligence efforts related to US elections have primarily focused on foreign intelligence collection. For decades, Russian and Soviet intelligence services have sought to collect insider information from US political parties that could help Russian leaders understand a new US administration's plans and priorities.

- The Russian Foreign Intelligence Service (SVR) Directorate S (Illegals) officers arrested in the United States in 2010 reported to Moscow about the 2008 election.

- In the 1970s, the KGB recruited a Democratic Party activist who reported information about then-presidential hopeful Jimmy Carter's campaign and foreign policy plans, according to a former KGB archivist.

Election Operation Signals "New Normal" in Russian Influence Efforts

We assess Moscow will apply lessons learned from its campaign aimed at the US presidential election to future influence efforts in the United States and worldwide, including against US allies and their election processes. We assess the Russian intelligence services would have seen their election influence campaign as at least a qualified success because of their perceived ability to impact public discussion.

- Putin's public views of the disclosures suggest the Kremlin and the intelligence services will continue to consider using cyber-enabled disclosure operations because of their belief that these can accomplish Russian goals relatively easily without significant damage to Russian interests.

- Russia has sought to influence elections across Europe.

We assess Russian intelligence services will continue to develop capabilities to provide Putin with options to use against the United States, judging from past practice and current efforts. Immediately after Election Day, we assess Russian intelligence began a spearphishing campaign targeting US Government employees and individuals associated with US think tanks and NGOs in national security, defense, and foreign policy fields. This campaign could provide material for future influence efforts as well as foreign intelligence collection on the incoming administration's goals and plans.

Annex A

Russia -- Kremlin's TV Seeks To Influence Politics, Fuel Discontent in US[*]

RT America TV, a Kremlin-financed channel operated from within the United States, has substantially expanded its repertoire of programming that highlights criticism of alleged US shortcomings in democracy and civil liberties. _The rapid expansion of RT's operations and budget and recent candid statements by RT's leadership point to the channel's importance to the Kremlin as a messaging tool and indicate a Kremlin-directed campaign to undermine faith in the US Government and fuel political protest._ _The Kremlin has committed significant resources to expanding the channel's reach, particularly its social media footprint._ _A reliable UK report states that RT recently was the most-watched foreign news channel in the UK._ _RT America has positioned itself as a domestic US channel and has deliberately sought to obscure any legal ties to the Russian Government._

In the runup to the 2012 US presidential election in November, English-language channel RT America -- created and financed by the Russian Government and part of Russian Government-sponsored RT TV (see textbox 1) -- intensified its usually critical coverage of the United States. The channel portrayed the US electoral process as undemocratic and featured calls by US protesters for the public to rise up and "take this government back."

- RT introduced two new shows -- "Breaking the Set" on 4 September and "Truthseeker" on 2 November -- both overwhelmingly focused on criticism of US and Western governments as well as the promotion of radical discontent.

- From August to November 2012, RT ran numerous reports on alleged US election fraud and voting machine vulnerabilities, contending that US election results cannot be trusted and do not reflect the popular will.

- In an effort to highlight the alleged "lack of democracy" in the United States, RT broadcast, hosted, and advertised third-

Messaging on RT prior to the US presidential election (RT, 3 November)

party candidate debates and ran reporting supportive of the political agenda of these candidates. The RT hosts asserted that the US two-party system does not represent the views of at least one-third of the population and is a "sham."

---

[*] This annex was originally published on 11 December 2012 by the Open Source Center, now the Open Source Enterprise.

- RT aired a documentary about the Occupy Wall Street movement on 1, 2, and 4 November. RT framed the movement as a fight against "the ruling class" and described the current US political system as corrupt and dominated by corporations. RT advertising for the documentary featured Occupy movement calls to "take back" the government. The documentary claimed that the US system cannot be changed democratically, but only through "revolution." After the 6 November US presidential election, RT aired a documentary called "Cultures of Protest," about active and often violent political resistance (RT, 1-10 November).

RT new show "Truthseeker" (RT, 11 November)

RT Conducts Strategic Messaging for Russian Government

RT's criticism of the US election was the latest facet of its broader and longer-standing anti-US messaging likely aimed at undermining viewers' trust in US democratic procedures and undercutting US criticism of Russia's political system. RT Editor in Chief Margarita Simonyan recently declared that the United States itself lacks democracy and that it has "no moral right to teach the rest of the world" (*Kommersant*, 6 November).

- Simonyan has characterized RT's coverage of the Occupy Wall Street movement as "information warfare" that is aimed at promoting popular dissatisfaction with the US Government. RT created a *Facebook* app to connect Occupy Wall Street protesters via social media. In addition, RT featured its own hosts in Occupy rallies ("Minaev Live," 10 April; RT, 2, 12 June).

- RT's reports often characterize the United States as a "surveillance state" and allege widespread infringements of civil liberties, police brutality, and drone use (RT, 24, 28 October, 1-10 November).

Simonyan steps over the White House in the introduction from her short-lived domestic show on REN TV (REN TV, 26 December 2011)

- RT has also focused on criticism of the US economic system, US currency policy, alleged Wall Street greed, and the US national debt. Some of RT's hosts have compared the United States to Imperial Rome and have predicted that government corruption and "corporate greed" will lead to US financial collapse (RT, 31 October, 4 November).

RT broadcasts support for other Russian interests in areas such as foreign and energy policy.

- RT runs anti-fracking programming, highlighting environmental issues and the impacts on public health. This is likely reflective of the Russian Government's concern about the impact of fracking and US natural gas production on the global energy market and the potential challenges to Gazprom's profitability (5 October).

- RT is a leading media voice opposing Western intervention in the Syrian conflict and blaming the West for waging "information wars" against the Syrian Government (RT, 10 October-9 November).

RT anti-fracking reporting (RT, 5 October)

- In an earlier example of RT's messaging in support of the Russian Government, during the Georgia-Russia military conflict the channel accused Georgians of killing civilians and organizing a genocide of the Ossetian people. According to Simonyan, when "the Ministry of Defense was at war with Georgia," RT was "waging an information war against the entire Western world" (*Kommersant*, 11 July).

In recent interviews, RT's leadership has candidly acknowledged its mission to expand its US audience and to expose it to Kremlin messaging. However, the leadership rejected claims that RT interferes in US domestic affairs.

- Simonyan claimed in popular arts magazine *Afisha* on 3 October: "It is important to have a channel that people get used to, and then, when needed, you show them what you need to show. In some sense, not having our own foreign broadcasting is the same as not having a ministry of defense. When there is no war, it looks like we don't need it. However, when there is a war, it is critical."

- According to Simonyan, "the word 'propaganda' has a very negative connotation, but indeed, there is not a single international foreign TV channel that is doing something other than promotion of the values of the country that it is broadcasting from." She added that "when Russia is at war, we are, of course, on Russia's side" (*Afisha*, 3 October; *Kommersant*, 4 July).

- TV-Novosti director Nikolov said on 4 October to the Association of Cable Television that RT builds on worldwide demand for "an alternative view of the entire world." Simonyan asserted on 3 October in *Afisha* that RT's goal is "to make an alternative channel that shares information unavailable elsewhere" in order to "conquer the audience" and expose it to Russian state messaging (*Afisha*, 3 October; *Kommersant*, 4 July).

- On 26 May, Simonyan tweeted with irony: "Ambassador McFaul hints that our channel is interference with US domestic affairs. And we, sinful souls, were thinking that it is freedom of speech."

RT Leadership Closely Tied to, Controlled by Kremlin

RT Editor in Chief Margarita Simonyan has close ties to top Russian Government officials, especially Presidential Administration Deputy Chief of Staff Aleksey Gromov, who reportedly manages political TV coverage in Russia and is one of the founders of RT.

- Simonyan has claimed that Gromov shielded her from other officials and their requests to air certain reports. Russian media consider Simonyan to be Gromov's protege (*Kommersant*, 4 July; Dozhd TV, 11 July).

- Simonyan replaced Gromov on state-owned Channel One's Board of Directors. Government officials, including Gromov and Putin's Press Secretary Peskov were involved in creating RT and appointing Simonyan (*Afisha*, 3 October).

- According to Simonyan, Gromov oversees political coverage on TV, and he has periodic meetings with media managers where he shares classified information and discusses their coverage plans. Some opposition journalists, including Andrey Loshak, claim that he also ordered media attacks on opposition figures (*Kommersant*, 11 July).

*Simonyan shows RT facilities to then Prime Minister Putin. Simonyan was on Putin's 2012 presidential election campaign staff in Moscow (*Rospress, 22 September 2010*, Ria Novosti, 25 October 2012*).

The Kremlin staffs RT and closely supervises RT's coverage, recruiting people who can convey Russian strategic messaging because of their ideological beliefs.

- The head of RT's Arabic-language service, Aydar Aganin, was rotated from the diplomatic service to manage RT's Arabic-language expansion, suggesting a close relationship between RT and Russia's foreign policy apparatus. RT's London Bureau is managed by Darya Pushkova, the daughter of Aleksey Pushkov, the current chair of the Duma Russian Foreign Affairs Committee and a former Gorbachev speechwriter (*DXB*, 26 March 2009; *MK.ru*, 13 March 2006).

- According to Simonyan, the Russian Government sets rating and viewership requirements for RT and, "since RT receives budget from the state, it must complete tasks given by the state." According to Nikolov, RT news stories are written and edited "to become news" exclusively in RT's Moscow office (Dozhd TV, 11 July; *AKT*, 4 October).

- In her interview with pro-Kremlin journalist Sergey Minaev, Simonyan complimented RT staff in the United States for passionately defending Russian positions on the air and in social media. Simonyan said: "I wish you could see...how these guys, not just on air, but on their own social networks, *Twitter*, and when giving interviews, how they defend the positions that we stand on!" ("Minaev Live," 10 April).

RT Focuses on Social Media, Building Audience

RT aggressively advertises its social media accounts and has a significant and fast-growing social media footprint. In line with its efforts to present itself as anti-mainstream and to provide viewers alternative news content, RT is making its social media operations a top priority, both to avoid broadcast TV regulations and to expand its overall audience.

- According to RT management, RT's website receives at least 500,000 unique viewers every day. Since its inception in 2005, RT videos received more than 800 million views on *YouTube* (1 million views per day), which is the highest among news outlets (see graphics for comparison with other news channels) (*AKT*, 4 October).

- According to Simonyan, the TV audience worldwide is losing trust in traditional TV broadcasts and stations, while the popularity of "alternative channels" like RT or Al Jazeera grows. RT markets itself as an "alternative channel" that is available via the Internet everywhere in the world, and it encourages interaction and social networking (*Kommersant*, 29 September).

- According to Simonyan, RT uses social media to expand the reach of its political reporting and uses well-trained people to monitor public opinion in social media commentaries (*Kommersant*, 29 September).

- According to Nikolov, RT requires its hosts to have social media accounts, in part because social media allows the distribution of content that would not be allowed on television (*Newreporter.org*, 11 October).

- Simonyan claimed in her 3 October interview to independent TV channel Dozhd that Occupy Wall Street coverage gave RT a significant audience boost.

The Kremlin spends $190 million a year on the distribution and dissemination of RT programming, focusing on hotels and satellite, terrestrial, and cable broadcasting. The Kremlin is rapidly expanding RT's availability around the world and giving it a reach comparable to channels such as Al Jazeera English. According to Simonyan, the United Kingdom and the United States are RT's most successful markets. RT does not, however, publish audience information.

- According to market research company Nielsen, RT had the most rapid growth (40 percent) among all international news channels in the United States over the past year (2012). Its audience in New York tripled and in Washington DC grew by 60% (*Kommersant*, 4 July).

- RT claims that it is surpassing Al Jazeera in viewership in New York and Washington DC (*BARB*, 20 November; RT, 21 November).

- RT states on its website that it can reach more than 550 million people worldwide and 85 million people in the United States; however, it does not publicize its actual US audience numbers (RT, 10 December).

TV News Broadcasters: Comparative Social Media Footprint

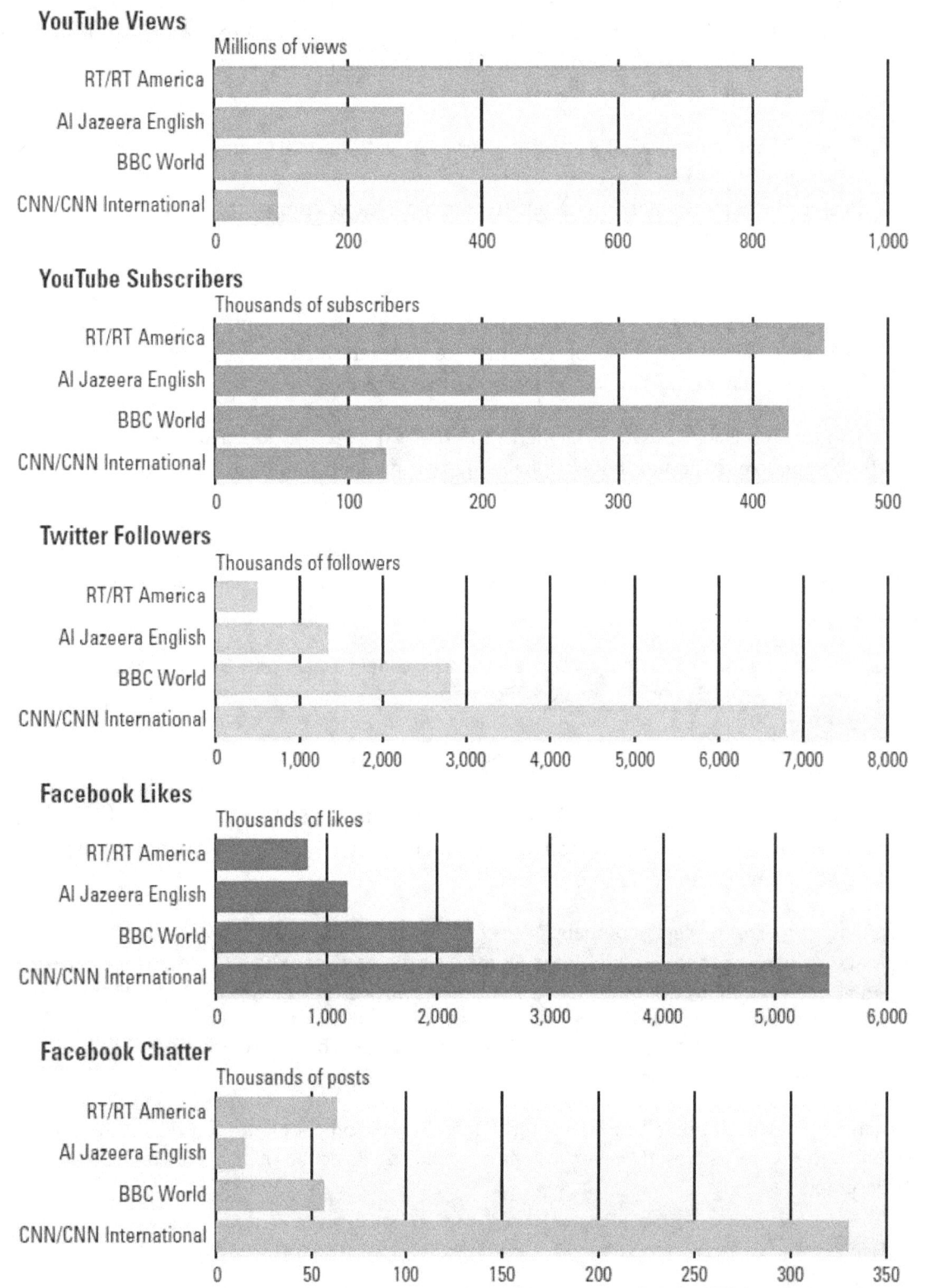

YouTube Views
Millions of views

YouTube Subscribers
Thousands of subscribers

Twitter Followers
Thousands of followers

Facebook Likes
Thousands of likes

Facebook Chatter
Thousands of posts

Formal Disassociation From Kremlin Facilitates RT US Messaging

RT America formally disassociates itself from the Russian Government by using a Moscow-based autonomous nonprofit organization to finance its US operations. According to RT's leadership, this structure was set up to avoid the Foreign Agents Registration Act and to facilitate licensing abroad. In addition, RT rebranded itself in 2008 to deemphasize its Russian origin.

- According to Simonyan, RT America differs from other Russian state institutions in terms of ownership, but not in terms of financing. To disassociate RT from the Russian Government, the federal news agency RIA Novosti established a subsidiary autonomous nonprofit organization, TV-Novosti, using the formal independence of this company to establish and finance RT worldwide (Dozhd TV, 11 July).

- Nikolov claimed that RT is an "autonomous noncommercial entity," which is "well received by foreign regulators" and "simplifies getting a license." Simonyan said that RT America is not a "foreign agent" according to US law because it uses a US commercial organization for its broadcasts (*AKT*, 4 October; *Dozhd TV*, 11 July).

- Simonyan observed that RT's original Russia-centric news reporting did not generate sufficient audience, so RT switched to covering international and US domestic affairs and removed the words "Russia Today" from the logo "to stop scaring away the audience" (*Afisha*, 18 October; *Kommersant*, 4 July).

- RT hires or makes contractual agreements with Westerners with views that fit its agenda and airs them on RT. Simonyan said on the pro-Kremlin show "Minaev Live" on 10 April that RT has enough audience and money to be able to choose its hosts, and it chooses the hosts that "think like us," "are interested in working in the anti-mainstream," and defend RT's beliefs on social media. Some hosts and journalists do not present themselves as associated with RT when interviewing people, and many of them have affiliations to other media and activist organizations in the United States ("Minaev Live," 10 April).

Annex B

ESTIMATIVE LANGUAGE

Estimative language consists of two elements: judgments about the likelihood of developments or events occurring and levels of confidence in the sources and analytic reasoning supporting the judgments. Judgments are not intended to imply that we have proof that shows something to be a fact. Assessments are based on collected information, which is often incomplete or fragmentary, as well as logic, argumentation, and precedents.

Judgments of Likelihood. The chart below approximates how judgments of likelihood correlate with percentages. Unless otherwise stated, the Intelligence Community's judgments are not derived via statistical analysis. Phrases such as "we judge" and "we assess"—and terms such as "probable" and "likely"—convey analytical assessments.

Percent

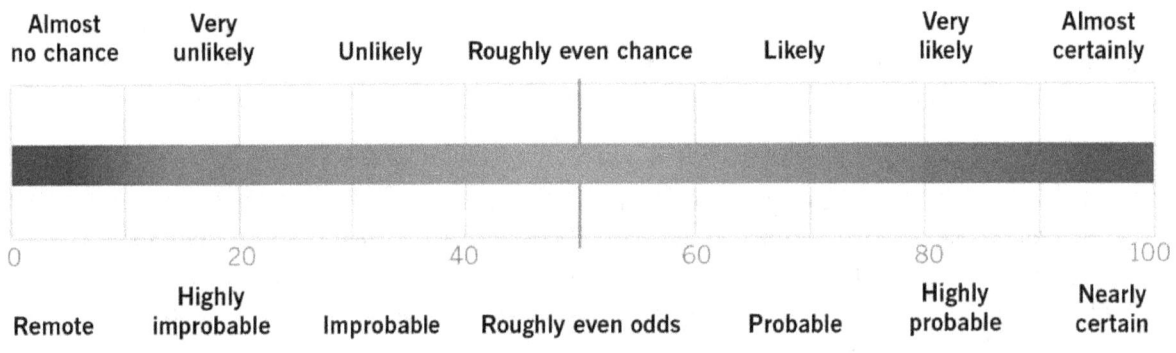

Almost no chance	Very unlikely	Unlikely	Roughly even chance	Likely	Very likely	Almost certainly
0	20	40	60	80	100
Remote	Highly improbable	Improbable	Roughly even odds	Probable	Highly probable	Nearly certain

Confidence in the Sources Supporting Judgments. Confidence levels provide assessments of the quality and quantity of the source information that supports judgments. Consequently, we ascribe high, moderate, or low levels of confidence to assessments:

- **High confidence** generally indicates that judgments are based on high-quality information from multiple sources. High confidence in a judgment does not imply that the assessment is a fact or a certainty; such judgments might be wrong.

- **Moderate confidence** generally means that the information is credibly sourced and plausible but not of sufficient quality or corroborated sufficiently to warrant a higher level of confidence.

- **Low confidence** generally means that the information's credibility and/or plausibility is uncertain, that the information is too fragmented or poorly corroborated to make solid analytic inferences, or that reliability of the sources is questionable.